Bad Habits

How to Turn Negative Habits Into Good Habits That Will Completely Turn Your Life Around

Robert S. Lee

Contents

Introduction

Smoking, skipping breakfast, and procrastinating, these are some of the habits that we all know we should change and erase from our lives. However, even if changing these habits have been a part of your resolution list for so many New Years', it's still hard to let these habits go. Well, let me tell you that it is going to change now.

You see, many people dream of changing their old ways, but most haven't really gotten into making the actual move to change. Don't be like that person; it's never too late to change; let this book help you.

This book contains proven steps and strategies that will show you how you can turn negative or bad habits into good habits. Why is habit change important, you ask? That's because habits run our lives!

You may not realize it, but habits play a huge role in our everyday lives. It transforms and shapes our lives either for the better or worse. To become the best you, you must stop looking at the big picture and start working on the small yet important stuff—your habits.

Through the pages of this book, you will be able to discover some negative habits that you may not be aware of. Identifying these habits is important because these are some of the probable reasons why you still haven't received the promotion you've been waiting for, or why you kept on breaking your New Year's resolutions.

This book also has a list of some of the good habits you should make in order to create a happy and satisfying life that you've always wanted. I've also included a list of some of the habits you can create to be more productive in the office. As a bonus, I've dedicated a chapter in this book to how habits and routine work together to make our lives better. But the most important of all, this book contains practical steps that you should follow in order to erase a bad habit and replace it with a good one.

Are you ready to start working on the new you?

Chapter 1. The Important Role of Habits in Our Lives

Have you ever thought about the power of habits? How it can either make or break you? And how it brought you to where you are today?

Even though you're now at the top of your game, or if you're still struggling to get there, habits are essential determinants of how our lives are today and how they will turn out in the future.

You see, the things we repeatedly do every day, the unconscious decisions and spontaneous actions we make are all habits. A study at Duke

University says that 40% of our actions or routines are made out of habits; and not because of the decisions we consciously make.

Can you imagine how your brain would feel if every movement you make, you did consciously? Without habits, our brain would be on overdrive, that even a simple task of brushing your teeth will take too much effort. How about riding a bike? If we're not able to create a habit, even a short-distance ride would be mentally exhausting because our brain is thinking too many things at the same time—how to balance the bike, use the pedals, avoid the bumps in the road, etc. Habits are there so that our brain can perform day-to-day tasks effortlessly.

How are habits formed?

According to research done at MIT in the 1990's, scientists have concluded that the basal ganglia, a certain part of the brain, is responsible for creating habits. When we do tasks or respond to stimuli repetitively, the brain is able to identify that pattern thus creating a habit. The basal ganglia is the reason why you automatically turn off the light when you go out of the room, why you say "thank you" when you're given a favor, and why you reach for that cigarette stick after every meal. Because of habits, we are able to accomplish tasks without putting much effort into it. Because of it, it leaves the cerebral cortex, also a part of the brain, to focus on the important things such as decision making and planning.

The Positive and the Negative

Yes, habits are a big part of our daily lives because they are responsible for accomplishing daily tasks seamlessly. However, even though habits make our lives easier, you must understand that habits have two different faces—the good and the bad. Obviously, good habits are the ones that help us respond to situations properly, maintain and build relationships with other people, and over-all just help us become a better person. Some examples of good habits are eating healthy, exercising, and being grateful. Bad habits, however, are the ones that hinder us in achieving our goals. Slacking around all day, drinking too much alcohol, and lying are just some of the negative habits that we all should erase from our lives.

Creating Good Habits for Success

Given that habits could shape our lives for the better or for the worse, we all must be mindful of the habits we make and maintain. If it's a successful life you want to achieve then you must start working on your habits.

To fully appreciate what I'm trying to point out, let me break it down to you this way: For example, your life goal right now is to finish college. Of course finishing a degree won't just fall into your lap; no. You have to work for it and earn it. So what do you do? You develop good studying habits. You lessen your nights out with your friends and spend more time reviewing for tests. You cut your video gaming hours short so that you will have enough time to work on your research paper. Making good habits are important because it helps you reach your goals!

In fact, the American Psychological Association has published a study saying that creating good habits are more important than goal-setting. They say that when people try to achieve their goals they use self-control and motivation to keep on going. However, when things don't go as planned people most of the time lose control and get back to their old ways. Creating habits, on the other hand, will keep you on track because that habit is already imbedded in your mind.

For example, one of your goals this year is to lose weight. However, you can't seem to control your habit of munching on every chocolate your hand will land on every time you're stressed. What do you do to achieve your goal? The first step is to erase that habit of stress eating and second, make it a habit of hitting the gym after work without any excuses. If you do this, I'm pretty sure that you'll be able to lose weight in no time.

I want to remind you, however, that it takes patience and perseverance to create a habit and break old ones. But the good news is it's possible! Continue reading this book and I'll tell you how!

"We are what we repeatedly do. Excellence, then, is not an act, but a habit."

~Aristotle

Chapter 2. 15 Negative Habits that are Holding You Back

Do you feel like you deserve a better life? Do you think that your efforts in the office are useless because your boss can't seem to recognize your contribution at work? Or, do you feel like you're a failure in many aspects of your life?

If your answer is "Yes" to one of these questions, then I'd like to ask you this: "Have you ever tried evaluating your habits to see if these are holding you back?" That's right. Habits play a huge role that determines where we are now, and where we'll be in the future. That's why it's important for you to be mindful of your habits and start replacing negative habits with positive habits.

If you think you're ready to change your life, then I'd like you to evaluate yourself. See if you recognize yourself having these negative habits I will mention below.

1. Procrastinating

I'm pretty sure that you will agree that most people are guilty of procrastination. You may think that putting things off won't have too much effect on your life, however, procrastination means wasted time; and wasted time means opportunities are passing you by.

2. Being the "Yes" man

You think that always saying "Yes" to your boss could give you a promotion, right? Well, this is true at some point, until the tasks or favors are too much to handle, causing you to fail and disappoint. Don't be afraid to say "No," especially if you feel like you have too much on your plate.

Don't bite off more than you can chew!

3. Being a perfectionist

Yes, it's OK to strive for perfection. However, if you often feel like everything has to be perfect and that everybody should give you the results that you expect then it will become a problem. Don't be afraid to fail. If things are always perfect then there will be no chance for you to grow and learn from your mistakes.

4. Multi-tasking

This is quite surprising, right? Although some people swear that multi-tasking helps them accomplish a lot of things at the same time, experts disagree and believe that multi-tasking can cause you to produce low-quality results. This is because the brain can only take so much at a time. You will be more productive, and produce outstanding results if you try to focus and take on things one at a time.

5. Seeing the glass half empty

Pessimism or always thinking negatively is the number one reason why you are not enjoying life. Not only that, being

pessimistic could also affect your
relationships and even worse, take a toll
on your health. According to experts,
harboring negative thoughts can affect
your immune system, which will make
you vulnerable to developing health
problems such as anxiety and
depression.

6. Lying

Some of us think that lying or covering
up the truth could get us out of trouble.
But I'm sure that we both know that
lying could mean bigger problems for us
especially if we're caught. Remember,
it's always easier to tell the truth than to
remember a lie.

7. Caring too much about other peoples' opinions

It's fine to listen or solicit advice from other people once in a while. However, if you care too much what others think you might just forget what matters to you most. It's OK to listen to the opinions of others, but always remember that you are in charge of your life. You will still be the only one who will face the consequences of the things you do in your life.

8. Being impulsive

Being impulsive could mean that you will be making decisions that you will regret in the future. One example of being impulsive is being carried away by the "sale" craze. Even if you think you're getting a bargain when you buy things on sale, it doesn't always mean that you need them at that moment. Before buying anything out of impulse, take a minute to think if the item you will be buying is the one you need. That way you won't be ending up with a dresser cluttered with things that you won't even use.

9. Drinking alcohol and smoking

This is a given and yet a lot of people drink too much, while others feel like they can't live without smoking. But you have to think about the costs of these vices. Doctors say that smoking even a single cigarette stick a day could cause plaque to buildup in your blood vessels and the arteries of your heart. Too much drinking (more than one bottle of beer a day for women and two bottles of beer for men) can lead to liver problems, high blood pressure, and even cancer.

10.   Not getting enough sleep

Getting enough good night's sleep (6-8 hours) is what most of people today lack. Even though you feel like a cup of espresso could give you energy to last throughout the day, even if you hadn't had enough sleep, getting quality snooze is important for health. Not only does it affect your energy levels and concentration, not having enough sleep could weaken your immune system, which makes you susceptible to different kinds of diseases.

11. Binging on junk food

I know that you already know that binging on foods that are laden with fat and sugar can cause harm to your health. Yes, you may feel satiated after eating a bag of chips, but these types of foods are called "empty calorie foods," they have zero vitamins and minerals, which means you're only eating what the name suggests—junk.

And because these foods have too much sugar and contain a lot of bad fat, eating them could increase your cholesterol levels, which could cause diabetes and heart disease.

12. Mindless eating

When most people are stressed, they tend to mindlessly crave for food, even if they are not hungry. Experts call this stress eating. The downside of this, however, is that most individuals crave for comfort food, a.k.a. empty calorie foods. Stress eating in the long run can

cause you to gain weight and be
vulnerable to other health problems
because of the high fat and sugar of
comfort foods.

13. Skipping breakfast

No, a cup of grande caramel macchiato
from Starbucks doesn't count as
breakfast. If you just drink coffee for
breakfast or skip it entirely, then you are
missing out on the most important meal
of the day. Eating nutritious food for
breakfast is essential because it gives
your body enough fuel to burn for
energy. When you skip breakfast, you
tend to eat more for lunch, during snack
time, or dinner, which can likely lead to
weight gain.

14. Not drinking enough water

Other than eating breakfast, this is another habit that most people overlook. Remember that the body is made up of 66% water, which means it needs enough supply of liquids for it to be in top shape. Doctors recommend drinking eight, 8 oz. glasses per day. Without drinking enough water our body will be dehydrated, which will cause fatigue. Other than that, it can also cause problems in the digestive system, ulcers, and weight gain.

15. Spending too much time in front of the TV

Spending too much time in front of the TV and slouching on the couch for almost a day could put you at risk of eye and heart problems. According to studies, slacking around the TV could increase the chances of being overweight or becoming obese; which we all know are health problems that can lead to other more serious illnesses. It can also strain and damage the eyes, which will also cause problems with your eyesight.

Are you guilty of at least one of the bad habits I mentioned above? I hope that this list was able to help you realize what habits you need to erase in your life. Now that you know the habits you need to change, the next chapter will discuss the habits that you need to develop.

Chapter 3. 15 Good Habits to Improve Your Life

As I've said earlier, habits make the most of what we do in our lives. That's why, if you want to create a positive change in your life or achieve your life's goals, then you should start working on developing good habits.

Listed below are some examples of good habits that I'm sure will propel you towards the direction you want your life to go.

1. Have a vision

I'm not sure about you, but I totally believe in the law of attraction. That whatever we set our minds to, it will surely happen in our lives. That's why, if you have a goal, for example, to be a top manager in your company, then what I suggest you do is allot a time in your day where you will visualize yourself attaining your goal. Imagine yourself having an office of your own, calling out the decisions your company, and most importantly, feeling contented with the career success you've achieved. The more you do this, the more you will be motivated to work on your goal.

2. Learn to listen

One essential factor of effective communication is listening. Be reminded that listening is different from hearing. You may act like you hear the person you're talking to, but in reality you're just too busy with your thoughts.

How else will you learn from other people if you don't listen? That's why one of the habits that you should build is an ability to listen. When you actively listen, you just might get nuggets of wisdom that will help or inspire you to be successful.

3. Be kind to others

Some individuals who are too focused on their goals tend to trample on other people so that they can move forward on the ladder to success. Don't be that person.

Always show courtesy and kindness to other people, no matter if they are there to help you or not. Because of this, you will see yourself having a good reputation, gaining more friends and feeling great about yourself because you don't have any conflicts with anyone. Surely, good karma will be knocking on your door if you develop this habit.

4. Practice gratefulness

I've read one book in the past that talked about the secrets of successful people and after reading it, I was able to underscore one common habit that all these individuals had, and that's gratefulness. When you practice the habit of always saying thank you for things that are either big or small, you tend to feel good about yourself. Being grateful makes you realize how blessed you are, which will always put you in a positive mood. Other than that, psychology experts say that people who are grateful are those who sleep well at

night and have a strong and lasting
relationship with others.

5. Think positively

Compared to pessimists, people who
think positively are able to live a full life.
Of course problems will still come even if
you are a positive thinker. However,
what differentiates you from the others
is that you are able to find solutions to
the problem and cope with stress better
because you see the light that is at the
end of the tunnel. Other than this
benefit, studies show that positive
thinking is actually good for our health
because it reduces the risk of developing
cardiovascular diseases and other
psychological problems such as
depression.

6. Smile

I'm sure you've heard of the saying "It takes more muscles to smile than to frown." But this is actually not true. According to Dr. David Song from the University of Chicago Medical Center, it actually takes a minimum of 10 muscles to smile and six muscles to frown. But here's the truth, it actually takes lesser effort to smile than to frown because humans are in born with this ability that even blind babies are able to smile!

Other than that, did you know that even a fake smile could actually lift up your mood? The reason for that is because the brain that dictates our emotions doesn't actually know whether a smile is genuine or not. So just flexing those muscles you use for smiling could definitely make you feel happier—so make it a habit of flashing those pearly whites as often as you can!

7. Keep a routine

If being more productive is your goal then keeping a routine is the habit you need to build. Routines make our lives easier because you already have a set of tasks you need to do in a certain period of time. Following a routine means you get things done faster since you already know what's ahead of you, which also mean that you have a better control of your life.

(I will discuss more about routines on Chapter 7)

8. Exercise daily

Besides keeping us fit and keeping those extra pounds of fat at bay, having regular physical activity can actually give us a lot good things that are beneficial for our whole-being.

Studies show that regular exercise actually boosts a hormone called endorphin, which keeps us happy and in a good mood. Exercise is actually seen as a means to lessen the symptoms of depression. Other than that, physical activity is also proven to help boost brainpower and sharpen the memory which is important for individuals who are in their twilight years.

9. Eat healthy

This might seem surprising to you, but losing weight is actually 30% exercise and 70% diet. Running extended hours on the treadmill won't have much impact if you keep your poor diet that's made of unhealthy foods. That's why, if you want to lose weight, or just be healthy, then you should be careful in the type of foods you eat. The rule of thumb of dietitian-nutritionists for a healthy plate is to have many colors of fruits and vegetables on your meals accompanied by a healthy serving of protein and grains.

10.   Drink more water

As you know, doctors recommend drinking eight glasses or two liters of water (soda, coffee, or alcohol don't count) every day. That's because most of our body is made of water, and it needs an adequate amount of H_2O for it to function properly. If you're not into drinking water, here are just some of the health benefits that you're missing out on:

- Drinking water helps you think and concentrate better—that's because the brain is made up of 90% water, so it needs adequate amounts to remain sharp.

- Are you experiencing headaches? Don't reach for that pain reliever yet. Did you know that chugging down glasses of water could relieve and prevent headaches? That's because headaches are more often than not caused by dehydration, so drink lots of water every day!

- Also, drinking lots of water aids in flushing out toxin build up in our body through our sweat and urine. It therefore prevents us from getting illnesses that are caused by harmful toxins.

11. Get up early

Productivity experts say that people who get up at the crack of dawn tend to accomplish more things than individuals who stay in bed a little longer. That's because mornings are the time of the day when our body is refreshed and has the highest levels of energy, which makes finishing tasks easier.

12. Spending time to pray or meditate

Allotting time for prayer or meditation is important to keep in your daily routine. That's because this is the time of the day when you are able to reflect on the

33

things you've accomplished and the
things that you have yet to do. When you
practice this, you have a clear sense of
what you want for your life and which
direction you want to take.

13. Be updated

Staying informed and catching up on the
latest news is one habit that many
successful individuals in the world has.
Bill Gates, one of the richest men in the
world, makes it a point to get a dose of
daily news from the New York Times,
the Wall Street Journal, and the
Economist, which he reportedly reads
from cover to cover. In an interview with
Rolling Stones, President Barack Obama
said that he starts his day reading the
New York Times, Washington Post, and
also, the Wall Street Journal.

14. Spend quality time with family

No matter how busy you are, it's vital that you allot quality time for family in your schedule. Even if it means sharing a hearty breakfast or a sumptuous dinner together, spending a lay afternoon at the park, or cuddling in front of the television to watch the latest episodes of your favorite TV series, quality time is important.

Psychologists agree that spending time with your children could actually boost their self-esteem, help develop positive behaviors, create a strong connection between parents and kids, and most importantly of all, it creates happy memories.

15. De-clutter

Whether it be disposing of physical clutter (unused clothes, food stock that are already expired, growing piles of magazines), or turning away from emotional and mental clutter, de-cluttering is another habit that you should build; doing this will free you of the clutter that is overwhelming you and causing you stress. De-cluttering clears your mind and enables you to live in the "now."

There are actually a lot of good habits that we all must build, but of course I couldn't fit them all in this book. If you are ready to make a transformation in your life, then go on to the next chapter to see how you can change your habits from negative to positive.

Chapter 4. Good Habits in the Office to Improve Productivity

Besides the good habits I mentioned in the previous chapter, it will be helpful for you to know some of the habits that could improve your productivity, especially in the office. In this part of the book, I've compiled some of the best practices of the most successful people in the world.

1. **Arrive early**

   Do you want to know how executives are able to manage a whole lot of things on their plate? It's because they start working early. If you make it a point to arrive at least an hour early to the office, you get to enjoy the silence before everybody starts showing up for work. This is the best time for you to reflect, make important decisions, and meditate on your tasks ahead without being bombarded with so many distractions. Brett Yomark, CEO of New Jersey Nets makes it a point to be at his office as early as 4:30 in the morning where he sends motivational emails to his team.

2. "Eat that frog first"

The main reason why tasks aren't getting done in the office is because of procrastination. Motivational speaker and book author Brain Tracy suggests one method that's proven to beat procrastination is to "eat that frog" first thing in the morning. What Tracy means here is that in order to get the wheels turning, you must take on the "ugliest" or hardest frog (task) in the morning. After accomplishing that ugly task, you will see that every task will be easier afterwards.

3. Schedule clerical tasks in the afternoon

Studies about office productivity have concluded that a worker's will power to finish his/her tasks is highest in the morning, that's why it's more ideal to finish important things in the morning and tackle clerical tasks in the afternoon.

The creator of Dilbert, Scott Adams actually does this technique. In his book

"How to Fail at Almost Everything and Still Win Big," Adams said that he usually works on his sketches in the morning when his creativity is at its peak and he schedules other not-so-important tasks in the afternoon.

4. The Power Hour

As soon as you clock in at the office, you sit down at your desk and you stare at your computer monitor for a while. Feeling like you're still not ready for work, you spend your first few minutes browsing the net, reading the news, or answering not so important emails. After dillydallying for a while you notice that you've already spent one hour of your time. You suddenly realize that you've spent precious hours doing nothing instead of tackling the important task you're supposed to do right away. What do you do to avoid this?

Experts say that if you want to improve your productivity at work, then you must apply the "Power Hour." This technique is simply allotting one hour to totally committing on focusing on one task. Your full attention should be spent on accomplishing this task alone for 60 whole minutes. Meaning, there should be no answering emails or calls in between and definitely no potty or water breaks. "By doing this, you are forcing yourself to remain focused," says Kevin Fleming, founder of Startup Workout. I recommend that you schedule this first thing in the morning since, like I said, your brain and your energy is at its best during the morning.

5. Take breaks

If you think that skipping break time will make you more productive, think again. That's because our brain, like our muscles, needs to rest once in a while. If you've been thinking or been squeezing your creative juices for straight hours, your brain must be screaming for you to take a break. According to experts, even a five-minute break to recharge your brain will help a lot to renew your energy and creativity.

6. Clear your desk

A survey done at a staffing firm in the United States said that most employees associate messy desks with individuals who are irresponsible and cannot be trusted with any tasks. That's why if you want to create a professional image of your work place, it would be a nice idea if you kept your desk tidy. It'll be wise for you to schedule a desk clean up at the end of every week so that clutter won't be piling up in your workspace.

7. List it down

I just can't image my life without my to-do list. I don't know about you, but keeping a list of what tasks I need to do for the day is a big help for me because it makes me see what's ahead and what I still need to do. I've been practicing this habit for many years now, and I find it very effective. I recommend that you start doing it too.

8. Avoid distractions

Especially now that browsing your Facebook feed is made easier (thanks to your smartphone), keeping yourself focused on your tasks will be harder to do. However, developing a habit of disciplining yourself to consciously avoid distractions will help you a lot in being productive.

Chapter 5. Steps to Change Negative Habits into Positive Habits

By now you already know the important role of habits in our lives and how essential it is to build good habits if you want to live a happier life. What I want you to realize now is that habits are a result of our doing. Habits are not inborn; they are formed through our repetitive behavior towards a certain situation. But no matter how ingrained habits are in our lives, there is always the chance to change them. Meaning, there is a way to change negative to positive habits. Now the question is, how?

The Habit Loop

A study in MIT coined a term called "habit loop" which Charles Duhigg discussed in his book, "The Power of Habit" as a "simple neurological loop at the core of every habit."

The habit loop is made of three different parts, which are the **cue**, **routine**, and **reward**.

Researchers explain that that cue is a certain situation or circumstance that triggers the habit. Routine on the other hand is the action or behavior you respond towards the cue; while the reward is the "thing" that gives you satisfaction when you do the habit.

For example, every time Alex finishes eating lunch, he goes out to light a cigarette with his friends and then come back in to proceed with his usual work routine. Although he's not a heavy smoker, the doctor already advised Alex to quit smoking because he is at risk of developing asthma. What does he do?

In his book, Duhigg explains that in order to alter a habit, it's important that you are able to determine all parts of the habit loop.

According to him, the first step that you should do is to determine the routine. If you look at Alex's smoking habit loop, his routine would be to go out to light a cigarette. The second step would be identifying the reward. Is it satisfying his body's addiction to nicotine? Or he just enjoys the conversation he shares with friends who smoke with him?

Now the last step that Duhigg suggests is to identify the cue. What could be the "trigger" of Alex's habit of smoking after eating lunch? To determine a cue you have to look at the following categories: emotional state, location, time, people, as well as the response that immediately precedes the trigger.

If we look at Alex's habitual cue on smoking, the feeling of a full stomach might actually be the cause for him to go out to light a stick. Not because of his addiction to nicotine, but because he just wants a few extra minutes to spend before sitting back down on his desk.

Now if this is the case, Alex could actually quit smoking if he looked for other ways to distract him from lighting a stick. Instead of going out, he could probably spend a couple of minutes in the office to chat or listen to music to relax instead of going back directly to work. Of course, like other bad habits, it will probably take time before Alex can actually quit his habit of smoking. But identifying the components of his habit loop is important so that he will have more control of his actions.

If you want to change a habit, then I recommend you identify it using the habit loop. See what triggers you to act on the habit and then look for ways to alter it.

The 21-day Challenge

Maxwell Maltz, a plastic surgeon, published a book in 1960 entitled "Psyho-Cybernatics" which contains his observations on how his patients were able to adjust the changes in their body. According to him, his patients who have undergone alterations in their bodies like breast augmentation and rhinoplasty, were able to adapt to the change in their body after 21 days. He also observed his own behavior and saw that he too was able to adapt to change after 21 days. Because Maltz's theory became so phenomenal, self-help authors have based their thoughts on this idea and have concluded that a habit can be formed or altered in 21 days.

What most authors fail to realize is that Maltz's theory says that our adaptation to change, comes AFTER 21 days and not IN 21 days. Meaning, accomplishing 21 days of habit changing or building your habits will not actually assure you that the habit is already ingrained in the brain. However, I agree that 21 days is a good number to start working on changing your habits from negative to positive. So now I urge you to take on the 21-day challenge.

What I want you to do is, pick one bad habit you want to change. Don't worry, I won't ask you to start working on the bad habits you think are hard to quit. Start small.

After that you have to analyze your habit based on the habit loop and then create a plan on how you can control yourself when the habit cue shows itself.

During these days I want you to keep a calendar marked from day 1-21 where you will write down your thoughts about the change you are going through. You can also keep a journal if you want to. This is important because writing it down will help you monitor your accomplishments and will also keep you on track.

"If you do not pour water on your plant, what will happen? It will slowly wither and die. Our habits will slowly wither and die away if we do not give them an opportunity to manifest. You need not fight to stop a habit. Just don't give it an opportunity to repeat itself."

~Swami Satchidananda, "The Yoga Sutras"

Chapter 6. 10 Simple Tips to Maintain Good Habits

Now that you know how to work on changing your habits from bad to good, maintaining them is a whole different story. Yes, it will be easy to keep up with the change for a few days, or maybe a few weeks, however, as the time passes, expect that fighting the urge to quit the bad habit will be a harder battle. So what do you do to maintain these habits?

Here are some tips to help you:

1. Remind yourself the of the purpose

When you see yourself longing to puff another cigarette remind yourself why you are quitting in the first place. Is it because you want to start living healthy? Or is it because you don't want your child to see you getting addicted to vices? Whatever the reason is, it will help you a lot if you keep a reminder to yourself why you want to change your habits in the first place. Like what I mentioned in the previous chapter, writing a journal about your transformation will help keep you on track.

2. One habit at a time

Breaking and creating habits, even one habit, is hard. And if you attempt to break bad habits at the same time, then you are most likely to fail. Not all of us have the capacity to have a "total" lifestyle change. That's why if it's success you want, then I suggest that you keep it simple and take one habit at a time. Focus on one habit first and then go on to the next when you feel like you're ready.

3. Practice it daily

Remember that consistency is important to create a habit, so practice it daily! The connections in our brain that create habits become stronger when we do things repetitively. If you want to start a habit of waking up early, then do it consecutively for more than 21 days. After that, you'll see that getting up early from bed will not be a struggle anymore.

4. Commit to the 21-day challenge

If a lifetime change may seem daunting to you, you can start small by challenging yourself to a 21-day habit change. Take things one-step at a time. You will see that after this "conditioning phase" these behaviors/habits that you want to create will stick to you like glue.

5. Make no excuses

If your goal is to have a habit of daily exercise, then you should not entertain any excuses. Yes, it's hard to get up from the couch, especially if your favorite TV series in on. However, if you're really serious about the change you want in your life, then you have to commit to that goal.

6. Divert your attention

Bad habits are really hard to break, but it is however, possible to turn your back on them. For example, if you want to stop your habit of slouching on your couch in front of the TV for long periods of time, it will be easier for you to break this if you are able to find an activity that will divert your attention, like taking a walk outside. Not only will this help you break the bad habit, but walking and enjoying the outdoors can actually be good for your physical, emotional, and mental health.

7. Avoid temptation

Changing the way you eat will be tough if you let junk food still linger in your cupboard. To avoid the temptation of eating junk, why don't you purge your pantry and throw out any food that is considered unhealthy? And then after, go buy groceries to stock up on healthy and nutritious snacks.

8. Be persistent

Not all individuals will be successful in their first attempt of breaking a habit. I have a friend who tried to quit smoking so many times. But it was his persistency that enabled him to finally turn his back on his vice.

9. Ask for help

It will always be easier for you to face any challenges if you have someone supporting you. Why don't you encourage your partner or a friend to take the 21-day habit change with you? So that whenever you feel like you're losing track, you have someone to remind you of your goals.

10. Visualize

Finally, if you want to make a habit stick, then what you need to do is to visualize yourself actually changing the habit and already achieving your goal. For example, if you want to start living healthy, then visualize yourself eating the right food, exercising, and looking fit. If you do this, it will surely inspire you to keep on working to achieve the habit you want to maintain.

Chapter 7. Habits and Routines

All throughout this book we've discussed habits—bad habits that you should break, and good habits that you should make. Now the question is: What do you do with these habits? How do you actually apply them in your life?

The answer is simple: Create a routine around these habits!

As I've said earlier, routines make our lives easier because we can simply accomplish things automatically and flawlessly. But what are the other benefits of having a routine?

- **Allows you to focus**

Most people today are easily distracted especially because the Internet (the number one source of distractions, in my opinion) can be easily accessed. I know you might be guilty of spending too much time leisurely browsing on the net without realizing that precious time is ticking by.

Keeping a routine will help you avoid this and will help you focus on things that matter most. How? For example, if your routine at the office is to spend 9am-10am answering important emails then you know that that time should only be dedicated to that specific task.

- **You find time to do other things**

Most people who don't follow any routine usually find themselves juggling one task to another because they don't know which comes first. On the contrary, people who follow a routine can easily find time to do other things, like spend quality time with the family or start a hobby, because they already know how to manage their time properly; thanks to their routine.

- **Helps you sleep at night**

Some studies show that people who run their lives on routines actually have higher quality sleep than those who don't. That's because routines help you to make sure that things are done. You don't have to toss and turn on your bed at night wondering whether you've accomplished all the tasks you have to do because your routine is able to help you do things automatically.

- **Routines are great for children**

    Child psychologists say that children are more likely to grow up as responsible adults if they live in a household that is run by routines. That's because routines give them a sense of security, assurance, and structure, which is important for children.

    If your child is used to a routine of waking up early in the morning and having breakfast, then you save yourself from arguing with them to get up because routines help them improve or develop their cooperation and self-discipline.

Still not convinced? I could give you a long list of successful individuals who run (or ran) their lives on routines, but one of the most popular persons who follow a strict routine is the United States' Founding Father, Benjamin Franklin. How do you think Ben was able to balance his responsibilities as a politician, businessman, inventor, and a scientist? He stuck with a routine!

Ben starts his day at five in the morning, where he ate breakfast, washed, and reflected on the day ahead. Before going to work, Ben asked this question to himself, "What good shall I do this day?" At eight he was usually out to work until lunch at twelve noon. After an hour, Ben will go back to work until five. By six in the evening, he took things slowly and enjoyed listening to music and eating supper. Before turning in for the day at ten, Ben would ask another question, "What good have I done today?" After full seven hours of sleep, Ben would rise up again before the crack of dawn and do his routine all over again.

Now, as you start your own routine, here are some tips you can follow in order to create routine schedule that will work for you.

1. Be true to yourself

Create a routine that is realistic. If you can only spend eight hours in the office, then make sure that the routines and tasks you schedule fit in those hours. Do not spread yourself too thin because you can only do so much.

2. Be open to changes

Change is the only thing that is constant in our world, that's why your routine should be open to change. However, this should not give you the liberty to go against the plan. Just make sure that your routine is flexible enough for

changes that you will encounter along
the way.

3. Schedule breaks in between

You are not a robot. You need to take a
break, eat, and sleep. Our whole body,
including our brain, needs to unplug and
recharge to gain energy. Unless you want
to break down like any overused gadget,
then breaks should always be part of
your routine.

4. Utilize your most productive hours

While it's ideal to schedule your most
important tasks in the morning, I know
some individuals who work best at night.
If this is you, then I suggest that you
work your schedule around the hours
when you feel like you are most
productive. Identify the time of the day

when your energy and creativity is at its peak and then schedule your most important task during this time.

5. Know what's important

Since all of us can only do so much in a day, it's vital that you know which tasks you need to prioritize. I suggest that you identify your tasks and categorize them under "Urgent," "Important," and "Less Important." Tasks that fall under "Urgent" are those that are important enough that they need immediate attention, tasks under the "Important" category are those that need your attention but can wait, while tasks that are "Less Important" are those that you can either put off for a while, or delegate to other people.

Creating a routine that works for you may take a few trial and errors however, if you find one that fits you, you better make sure to stick to it.

Conclusion

I hope you were able to realize the importance of habits in our lives and how they can help us be successful. I trust that through this book, you were able to pinpoint bad habits that you need to erase and the good habits that you need to develop for a happier life. I wish you all the best as you start your journey into becoming the new and improved you.

Keep in mind that changing negative to positive habits is not easy, but it is worth it. Take the 21-day challenge today and see how altering habits can do wonders for your life. Stop procrastinating, do it now!

Good luck!

"Just do it! First you make you habits, then your habits make you!"

~Lucas Remmerswaal, The A-Z of 13 Habits: Inspired by Warren Buffet

www.ingramcontent.com/pod-product-compliance
Lightning Source LLC
Chambersburg PA
CBHW071246020426
42333CB00015B/1657